Nine Holy Hours
to Discern the Priesthood

VIANNEY VOCATIONS

Nine Holy Hours to Discern the Priesthood
By Sam Alzheimer
All rights reserved. Published 2022

© Vianney Vocations
Tallahassee, FL
Printed in the United States of America

ISBN: 978-1-7353293-6-9

Contents

Why & How to Use this Book

Jesus is about to speak to you.

If you're reading this book, you desire a clear answer about your vocation. You probably feel a strong natural desire for marriage and family, along with a spiritual desire—or at least an initial attraction—to the possibility of the priesthood.

You may be wishing that Jesus could visit you personally and tell you exactly what to do. If only he could just text you a clear plan for your life!

Actually, he can. He's been doing it for centuries. The personal visit is when you enter the chapel and kneel before the Blessed Sacrament. And the text isn't on your phone, but in your Bible.

If you give Jesus nine hours in the chapel, nine hours of fervent prayer, nine hours of serious mediation on the scriptures, he will speak.

> *"Ask and it will be given to you; seek and you will find; knock and the door will be opened to you. For everyone who asks, receives; and the one who seeks, finds; and to the one who knocks, the door will be opened." Mt. 7:7-8*

Jesus will speak to you. Believe that. Count on it.

The nine Holy Hours in this book are not about passive listening. Instead, you will be knocking, *loudly*, on the door of heaven. You will be actively engaging God's Word in the presence of God's Son. You will kneel before the Eucharist and beg the Lord for insights and answers.

At the same time, be realistic about yourself. No one has ever prayed intensely for nine hours without distractions. Your prayer will, at times, be imperfect. Don't worry if one or two Holy Hours are not particularly fruitful or inspiring. As you will discover, you may need only one good conversation with Jesus to change your life.

Structure of each Holy Hour

10 min **Focus Your Heart**
Kneel before the Lord and pray from the heart.

30 min **Contemplative Prayer**
Read the scripture and complete the contemplation.

20 min **Write**
Record the experience of prayer so you can review in the future.

Start each Holy Hour with "Trinity Minutes"

When you first enter the chapel and come before Our Lord, don't just sit there. (Sometimes this is okay, but not now. These Holy Hours are *active* prayer.) Instead, make an act of the will, a concerted effort to reorient yourself to the Trinity. Here is a simple formula to use:

- For one minute, praise God the Father and then thank him for one thing.
- For one minute, praise God the Son and then repent for one thing.
- For one minute, praise God the Holy Spirit and then ask for inspiration for your Holy Hour.

About Contemplative Prayer

The main part of each Holy Hour—the scripture reading and meditation—takes concentrated effort. You will not be skimming the scripture, but instead, reading it two, three, or even four times. In most of the Holy Hours, you will be asked to imagine yourself in the scene, perhaps as a spectator, perhaps as a main character. In some cases, you will be imagining a hypothetical future as a priest.

A word about this kind of imaginative prayer. St. Ignatius called it contemplation, a word that means "with color." The idea is to imagine every physical detail of the biblical scene. Engage all five senses: smell the spring air in Galilee, hear the squeak of leather sandals, see the deep red of wine, feel the rough texture of Christ's cloak, taste the tears running down your face.

You can go as far as you want in these "daydreams," letting your imagination wander off-script, filling in details and characters that are not explicitly in the biblical text. Importantly, you are not merely watching the scene; you must imagine yourself *in* the scene.

Some might say, "I'm not very imaginative; I'm not sure if I'll be good at this method of prayer." But you're probably better at it than you think. Consider that everyone can imagine what the future might hold; this is a distinguishing factor of being human. The God-given faculty of imagination is the reason that all people, in all of history, love stories. St. Ignatius, who made famous this method of prayer, knew the power of imagination. Over the centuries, tens of thousands of people, including hundreds of canonized saints, have followed Ignatius' method of contemplative, imaginative prayer. With a little practice, you can do it, too.

Important: The Colloquy

The highpoint of this imaginative prayer is what St. Theresa of Avila called the "colloquy" or conversation. The whole meditation should culminate in you speaking one-on-one with Jesus. For example, if you are meditating on the call of the disciples, even if the scene involves a crowd, you will imagine that somehow you find yourself alone with Jesus, having an intimate face-to-face conversation. It's like a movie scene in which time stops, everything else fades into the background, and only the main characters are moving and speaking. This is the pinnacle of prayer, the instant of insight, the privileged place of encounter with the Son of God. This is the "good stuff" of prayer.

Jesus is about to speak to you. You are about to be amazed at what he has to say.

HOLY HOUR 1

HEALING

In this Holy Hour, focus on the power of Jesus to heal you.

Everyone has sins, insecurities, and habits that cause pain and wound the soul. You can probably think of a few burdens right away. You might wish, "If I could only get rid of _____" or "If only _____ would have never happened."

In the scriptures we learn of someone else who had similar thoughts—the woman with the hemorrhage. She had a persistent medical condition that was ruining her life. And once she learned of Jesus, her only thought was: "If only I could touch his cloak."

Before reading the scripture, prepare by spending a few minutes thinking of the things in your life that need healing: anything that is burdening you from the past, any persistent habits or sins, any wounded relationships. Interiorly admit that you can't fix these things on your own. Admit that you need healing and grace from God. Now read the scripture.

The Healing of the Woman with the Hemorrhage
Mark 5:25-34

There was a woman afflicted with hemorrhages for twelve years. She had suffered greatly at the hands of many doctors and had spent all that she had. Yet she was not helped but only grew worse. She had heard about Jesus and came up behind him in the crowd and touched his cloak. She said, "If I but touch his clothes, I shall be cured." Immediately her flow of blood dried up. She felt in her body that she was healed of her affliction.

Jesus, aware at once that power had gone out from him, turned around in the crowd and asked, "Who has touched my clothes?" But his disciples said to him, "You see how the crowd is pressing upon you, and yet you ask, 'Who touched me?'" And he looked around to see who had done it. The woman, realizing what had happened to her, approached in fear and trembling. She fell down before Jesus and told him the whole truth. He said to her, "Daughter, your faith has saved you. Go in peace and be cured of your affliction."

Read the passage two or three times, memorizing the flow of events, and paying attention to details or phrases that stand out to you.

As described on page 9 in the Introduction, creatively imagine yourself in this scene using all five sense. First imagine your tremendous desire for healing. Recall how you've given up sometimes, but also how your wounds push you to great lengths to find wholeness. Imagine a busy town, jostling crowds, swirling rumors about the miracle-worker from Nazareth. See the scene—the rudimentary buildings, gnarled olive trees, the sky, the merchants shouting and the beggars pleading. Imagine what you are wearing, how long you have walked, the last time you ate. See the thicker crowds ahead on a small hill in the middle of town, surrounding Jesus. You are jostling your way toward the healer, the miracle-man, desperate to touch him, maybe even talk to him. Imagine the annoyed looks of those you push past, feel their elbows and hear their sharp words. Now you are close. See his sandals, his shabby grayish-brown cloak, torn in a few places. You reach out, crushed by the crowd, barely getting your arm between two bodies—and touch the edge of his cloak, just for an instant.

The world stands still. Light and power rush through you. You feel whole for the first time in years. Your chest is bursting with wonder, amazement. You suddenly understand that ancient emotion of "fear of the Lord."

But he knows. He's stopped and is asking his disciples about something. He's looking around, searching the crowd. There's nowhere to go, no retreat through the thick mass of bodies. He sees you and your eyes lock. Brown eyes, piercing but kind, intense and full of depth, seeing all the way through you. He's not angry. Time stops and the crowd disappears. It's just you and Jesus. You can tell he wants to talk. He's waiting for you to say something.

Colloquy

Thank Jesus for his healing power. With confidence, present to him all the areas of your life that need healing. Hear his words: "Go in peace and be cured of your affliction." Ask him about the other things on your heart. Ask him about your future. Listen intently. What else is he saying?

Write about your prayer

Use a notebook to write down your reflections. You may be tempted to skip writing, but your notes will be important later as you revisit your discernment process. Even if you don't write extensively, write enough to remind yourself of the key insights you gained.

1. Images. In this meditation, what was the most powerful thing you saw, heard, touched, smelled, or tasted? What did God show you through this?

2. Realizations. In reflecting on this passage; what did you realize that you did not understand or think about before?

3. Discernment. Based on insights in your mediation, where might Jesus be leading you? What are your options?

4. Resolutions. What is Jesus asking you to do, concretely and specifically, as a result of this meditation? What is your resolution? When and how will you do it?

CONVERSION

In this Holy Hour, focus on Jesus's invitation to radical change in your life. The word "conversion" means "turning around," or turning from one thing to face a new direction.

In preparation for your meditation, think about how you are profoundly influenced by the culture. Think about your upbringing, your schooling, your friends, your values. Acknowledge that in many ways, you are a man of this time and place. Even though you love God and the Church, admit that parts of you are still very worldly. Think about your media consumption, your attachment to sports or gaming. Recall the times that your interests have consumed you.

Ask the Lord to show you all these external influences in your life, the bad and the good. Try to see your own soul surrounded by various things vying for your attention. Name those things. Now read the scripture passage.

The Conversion of St. Paul

Acts 9:1-22

Now Saul, still breathing murderous threats against the disciples of the Lord, went to the high priest and asked him for letters to the synagogues in Damascus, that, if he should find any men or women who belonged to the Way, he might bring them back to Jerusalem in chains. On his journey, as he was nearing Damascus, a light from the sky suddenly flashed around him. He fell to the ground and heard a voice saying to him, "Saul, Saul, why are you persecuting me?" He said, "Who are you, sir?" The reply came, "I am Jesus, whom you are persecuting. Now get up and go into the city and you will be told what you must do."

The men who were traveling with him stood speechless, for they heard the voice but could see no one. Saul got up from the ground, but when he opened his eyes he could see nothing; so they led him by the hand and brought him to Damascus. For three days he was unable to see, and he neither ate nor drank.

There was a disciple in Damascus named Ananias, and the Lord said to him in a vision, "Ananias." He answered, "Here I am, Lord." The Lord said to him, "Get up and go to the street called Straight and ask at the house of Judas for a man from Tarsus named Saul. He is there praying, and in a vision he has seen a man named Ananias come in and lay his hands on him, that he may regain his sight." But Ananias replied, "Lord, I have heard from many sources about this man, what evil things he has done to your holy ones in Jerusalem. And here he has authority from the chief priests to imprison all who call upon your name." But the Lord said to him, "Go, for this man is a chosen instrument of mine to carry my name before Gentiles, kings, and Israelites and I will show him what he will have to suffer for my name."

So Ananias went and entered the house; laying his hands on him, he said, "Saul, my brother, the Lord has sent me, Jesus who appeared to you on the way by which you came, that you may regain your sight and be filled with the holy Spirit." Immediately things like scales fell from his eyes and he regained his sight. He got up and was baptized, and when he had eaten, he recovered his strength.

He stayed some days with the disciples in Damascus, and he began at once to proclaim Jesus in the synagogues, that he is the Son of God. All who heard him were astounded and said, "Is not this the man who in Jerusalem ravaged those who call upon this name, and came here expressly to take them back in chains to the chief priests?" But Saul grew all the stronger and confounded the Jews who lived in Damascus, proving that this is the Messiah.

Read the passage two or three times, memorizing the flow of events, and paying attention to details or phrases that stand out to you. As described on page 9 in the Introduction, creatively imagine yourself in this scene using all five senses.

In this meditation, perhaps see yourself as a companion of Saul. Like him, you feel the same zealous drive to punish people who deviate from the established religion. Imagine you have been tasked with preparing for the journey to Damascus: the food, water, and importantly, the chains in which to bind any Christians you find there. They clank heavily in your satchel as you set out with Saul on the dusty road. Imagine the conversation you have on the way, the determined look on Saul's face, his steel-like resolve.

Imagine a bend in the road in a remote place, halfway to your destination. Suddenly there is a tremendous blinding light, like ten bolts of lightning at once, searing the air around Saul. His body hits the ground, his limbs writhing in the dust. The loudest, deepest, most authoritative voice you have ever heard is speaking. You pick up Saul with the help of other companions, seeing his confidence utterly drained. You know exactly how he feels. The voice was unmistakable; there is no room for misinterpretation. You are certain it was Jesus. Suddenly the purpose of your trip, the purpose of your life, means nothing. The rest of the way to Damascus, the chains in your pack feel like they weigh a hundred pounds.

You are with Paul in a darkened room as he lays there, listless and blind. The last three days there's been a lot of time to think. The memory of the voice keeps resounding in your head.

A man comes. There is something different about him, a steady sureness as he speaks to Paul. Suddenly he is pouring water over Paul's head. He lays hands on Paul, invoking the Holy Spirit. Paul sits up, wide-eyed and alert, then stands, clearly restored back to full strength. Incredibly, he begins praising and thanking Jesus aloud. Inspired, you know the time has come. You, too, ask Ananias for baptism, and you feel the power of the Holy Spirit fill you.

Colloquy

Ananias and Paul leave the room, and you are seemingly alone, but you know Jesus is there. You feel his presence. You remember his words: "Go into the city and you will be told what you must do." Speak to him now. Ask him what to do. Repent of your attachment to worldly things, of your disinterest in holy things. Ask him what he wants in your new life. Ask him what to do about the chains.

Write about your prayer

Use a notebook to write down your reflections. Your notes will be very important later as you revisit your discernment process.

1. **Images.** In this meditation, what was the most powerful thing you saw, heard, touched, smelled, or tasted? What did God show you through this?

2. **Realizations.** In reflecting on this passage; what did you realize about the process of conversion?

3. **Discernment:** Pope Francis said, "Discipleship and discernment are two sides of the same coin." If you decide to follow Jesus with your whole heart, mind, and strength, things cannot continue "as-is." Converted disciples have to figure out not only what to do, but also what they must abandon. Can you see Jesus pointing toward a new path? What is it?

4. **Resolutions.** What is Jesus asking you to do, concretely and specifically, as a result of this meditation? Do you need to give up some sort of attachment? When and how will you do it?

THE CALL

In this Holy Hour, focus on the possibility of leaving a "regular" comfortable life.

In preparation for your meditation, think about your current life trajectory. Whether you're a student or working at a job, reflect on your optimal path forward. Think about your goals and plans. If you fast-forward five years, what does your "best life" look like?

After you've spent a few moments "daydreaming," ask yourself a critical question: is your vision of your "best life" also what's best for your soul? Now read the scripture.

The Call of Levi (Matthew)
Mark 2:13-17

Once again he went out along the sea. All the crowd came to him and he taught them. As he passed by, he saw Levi, son of Alphaeus, sitting at the customs post. He said to him, "Follow me." And he got up and followed him.

While he was at table in his house, many tax collectors and sinners sat with Jesus and his disciples; for there were many who followed him. Some scribes who were Pharisees saw that he was eating with sinners and tax collectors and said to his disciples, "Why does he eat with tax collectors and sinners?" Jesus heard this and said to them, "Those who are well do not need a physician, but the sick do. I did not come to call the righteous but sinners."

Read the passage two or three times. Note that Mark's Gospel tends to convey a lot of information in few words, so there may be more to the story than first meets the eye. Memorize the flow of events, paying attention to details or phrases that stand out to you. As described on page 9 in the Introduction, creatively imagine yourself in this scene using all five senses.

Imagine yourself as Levi (called Matthew in the other Gospels), sitting at your custom's post. You're at a desk on the porch of a nice little building, perched on a ridge above the Sea of Galilee. It's a beautiful day with a nice breeze coming off the water. There's sure to be a long procession of fisherman and traders today; revenue should be good. "Not a bad life," you think. Except, of course, it's not true. Most people hate you for gouging them on taxes. On the other hand, you do have a great house, eat the best food, and have some entertaining nights with the other tax collectors. It's pretty nice on the surface. Truth is, though, you're rich but lonely.

Feeling a bit melancholy, you gaze down the hill at a crowd gathered around a man who seems to be preaching or teaching. He must be telling stories, because you hear the whole crowd laugh. You can see whole families, even little kids, sitting rapt with attention. If you're honest, you'd rather be down there with them, listening, being part of something. You can tell this is no ordinary preacher. Something more than curiosity is growing in your heart.

Now the teacher is done and is walking up the hill followed by a few other men. He's striding like a man accustomed to long walks. He almost looks like he's coming your way. Wait, he *is* coming this way. He's taking the stone steps. Now he's right here, before you, his hands on your desk—weathered, calloused hands. He is leaning toward you, looking right into your eyes, with an intensity that is both terrifying and magnetic. He says two words, slowly, deliberately: "Follow me."

All at once, you know that this life, collecting shekels by the sea, is as meaningless as straw. Following this man is *real* life.

You get up from your desk, leaving all the money behind, unguarded. You've literally "left money on the table," something undreamt of for you. You're now walking right beside him. The whole town can see you, even the group of pharisees you pass along the road. "This is crazy. What am I doing?" you think, "Everyone knows who I am. Everyone knows I'm a fraud. Everyone knows I'm not good enough to be near this man."

Jesus seems to know where he's going; you certainly do. He motions to the gate and you unlock the latch with your key. As you do, you suddenly remember it's your turn tonight: the other tax collectors—your only companions these days—are all coming over, and they normally bring their female companions. This will be embarrassing.

But the dinner is like no other. As usual, the food is good, the wine flows, but Jesus changes everything. The conversation is not crude or banal, but meaningful, profound. Just to listen to his voice is to be transformed. You can barely believe this man is in your house, has made himself your friend—and now, as it's becoming clear, is inviting you to become a permanent part of his crew.

When the pharisees come, as they often do, with their jeers and insults, they direct them toward Jesus for a change. Whereas normally you feel guilty and angry when they confront you, Jesus's response is peaceful and measured: "Those who are well do not need a physician, but the sick do," then looking at you, he adds, "I did not come to call the righteous, but sinners."

Colloquy

The dinner ends without the usual carousing. Jesus and his disciples help clean up. Then it's just you and Jesus, there near the earthen fireplace. He looks at you expectantly. Everything is welling up in you at once: your life, your bad decisions, your loneliness. But is change even possible for you? Can you abandon this life, this course you're on? You have to say something. Talk it out, all of it. How does Jesus respond?

Write about your prayer

Use a notebook to write down your reflections. Your notes will be very important later as you revisit your discernment process.

1. Images. In this meditation, what was the most powerful thing you saw, heard, touched, smelled, or tasted? What did God show you through this?

2. Realizations. In reflecting on this passage, what observations did you make about the sacrifices of changing course in life?

3. Discernment. Is Jesus asking you to take a new direction in your life? Or at least adjust? How?

4. Resolutions. What is Jesus asking you to do, concretely and specifically, as a result of this meditation? When and how will you do it?

HOLY HOUR 4
PREACHING

In this Holy Hour, imagine being ordained a priest and preaching the gospel of Jesus Christ.

This Holy Hour is a bit different than the first three. It will involve two contemplations. The first is a daydream— a "holy fantasy"—about the day of your ordination if you were to become a priest. In the second meditation, you will imagine preaching a homily to the eighth-grade students in your parish.

Even if you're completely undecided about the priesthood, allow yourself for the next half-hour to imagine a hypothetical situation.

What would happen if you discerned that God was indeed calling you to the priesthood? Imagine contacting the Vocation Director, then sitting in his office talking about your life and God's call. He is friendly and warm and offers insightful counsel. He agrees that the Lord seems to be calling you. He guides you through the whole application, including a thorough examination by a psychologist. The whole process is eye-opening; you have never learned more about yourself than during these weeks!

Now fast-forward. You've been through six years of seminary. It was an amazing experience, not always easy, but far richer than you expected. You are a different man than when you began seminary—much more knowledgeable about Jesus, the Sacred Scriptures and the teaching of the Church. You have spent literally thousands of hours before the Blessed Sacrament. You are far more mature.

Finally, you are ordained by the bishop in your home diocese. Briefly picture this scene now: you are prostrate on the floor of the cathedral as the choir sings the Litany of Saints, praying that you will be a holy priest! See your bishop now, the successor to the apostles, as you kneel before him. He lays his hands upon your head and ordains you a priest of Jesus Christ. Take some time with this meditation.

Now imagine when the bishop assigns you to a parish. Make it the parish you know the best—either the one you are at now, or perhaps the parish where you grew up. You are the pastor now. Imagine all the details of your life here. See where you park your car. With your keys in hand, walk up the sidewalk to the rectory. Imagine training the altar servers, helping the youth group, saying an opening prayer at a parish dinner. Take a few moments to really fill in the details, using all five senses. Feel the roman collar on your neck. Smell the candles in the sacristy. Hear the church secretary calling down the hall to your office. This parish is your home, your life. These are your people. Pause and reflect on the experience of being the spiritual father of this family.

...

The eighth-grade catechist has asked you to lead a special Holy Hour for the students who are preparing for Confirmation. The theme is "Bold Witness to the World." It is a "sending-forth" as they prepare to be confirmed and soon enter high school. They've chosen a scripture for the meditation, and it's a long one. Read it with an eye for how you will preach on it:

Peter Cures the Crippled Man, Preaches about Jesus, and is Arrested
Acts 3:1-21, 4:1-4

Now Peter and John were going up to the temple area for

the three o'clock hour of prayer. And a man crippled from birth was carried and placed at the gate of the temple called "the Beautiful Gate" every day to beg for alms from the people who entered the temple. When he saw Peter and John about to go into the temple, he asked for alms. But Peter looked intently at him, as did John, and said, "Look at us." He paid attention to them, expecting to receive something from them.

Peter said, "I have neither silver nor gold, but what I do have I give you: in the name of Jesus Christ the Nazorean, rise and walk." Then Peter took him by the right hand and raised him up, and immediately his feet and ankles grew strong. He leaped up, stood, and walked around, and went into the temple with them, walking and jumping and praising God. When all the people saw him walking and praising God, they recognized him as the one who used to sit begging at the Beautiful Gate of the temple, and they were filled with amazement and astonishment at what had happened to him.

As he clung to Peter and John, all the people hurried in amazement toward them in the portico called "Solomon's Portico." When Peter saw this, he addressed the people, "You Israelites, why are you amazed at this, and why do you look so intently at us as if we had made him walk by our own power or piety? The God of Abraham, the God of Isaac, and the God of Jacob, the God of our ancestors, has glorified his servant Jesus whom you handed over and denied in Pilate's presence, when he had decided to release him. You denied the Holy and Righteous One and asked that a murderer be released to you. The author of life you put to death, but God raised him from the dead; of this we are witnesses. And by faith in his name, this man, whom you see and know, his name has made strong, and the faith that comes through it has given him this perfect health, in the presence of all of you. Now I know, brothers, that you acted out of ignorance, just as your leaders did; but God has thus brought to fulfillment what he had announced beforehand through the mouth of all the prophets, that his Messiah would suffer. Repent, therefore, and be converted, that your sins may be wiped away and that the Lord may grant you times of refreshment and send you the Messiah already appointed for you, Jesus, whom heaven must receive until the times of universal restoration of which God spoke through the mouth of his holy prophets from of old.

While they were still speaking to the people, the priests, the captain of the temple guard, and the Sadducees confronted them, disturbed that they were teaching the people and proclaiming in Jesus the resurrection of the dead. They laid hands on them and put them in custody until the next day, since it was already evening. But many of those who heard the word came to believe and the number of men grew to about five thousand.

Note that as you prepare the homily for the students, your task is the same as Peter's: to tell people about Jesus in a way that draws them into a relationship with the Savior. Do a "heart check" for a moment and compare yourself to Peter. Obviously from the story, the Holy Spirit was welling up inside him. As he strode into the temple area, he was truly "a man on a mission." He did not so much choose the words he preached as they came streaming out of him, out of a heart on fire for Jesus. When you think about the world today, the Church today, the brokenness of our society, what do you feel? Do you have a hunger to bring God's grace and truth so it can change to the world? Even if you are not ready right now, do you at least have a fundamental desire? Not a theoretical desire—that "someone" should spread the gospel. But do you have a desire to do it *personally*? If not, do you see how this desire could grow in you over time?

Now re-read the scripture again, looking for one or two phrases that the Holy Spirit is highlighting for you. Think about the message your young parishioners should hear.

Now the students come in. You bring the Blessed Sacrament out of the tabernacle and place Our Lord in the monstrance. After a period of silence, you stand at the ambo and proclaim the Gospel. Feel the pages as you turn them; look at the faces of the students. Hear your voice filling the church. Now ask the students to close their eyes and lead them through a meditation. What do you preach?

Colloquy

After the Holy Hour is over the students thank you as they shake your hand and leave for home. After they are gone, imagine sitting alone in the front pew of the empty church. You feel good about the message you've preached. You feel the Lord looking on you with approval, thanking you for your faithfulness: "Well done, my good and faithful servant." Basking in his love, have a heart-to-heart conversation with him about your life and future. Listen to his response.

Write about your prayer

Use a notebook to write down your reflections. Your notes will be very important later as you revisit your discernment process.

1. Images. In this meditation, what was the most powerful thing you saw, heard, touched, smelled, or tasted? What did God show you through this?

2. Realizations. In your meditation, did you realize anything new about the priesthood? Do you have any new understanding about preaching? When it comes to spreading the Gospel message, where is your heart?

3. Discernment: What insights did God give you about your vocation? What is a possible timeline for your next steps?

4. Resolutions. What is Jesus asking you to do, concretely and specifically, as a result of this meditation? When and how will you do it?

CONFESSION

In this Holy Hour, imagine hearing confessions as a priest. Not only that—imagine being sent by Jesus, personally, to forgive sins and heal souls.

This imaginative prayer will have two parts. In the first, you will encounter Jesus' own desire to heal, and his commissioning of the disciples to do likewise. In the second, you will imagine hearing the confession of a young man at an ordinary parish penance service.

As you read the following scripture, put yourself in the place of one of the apostles of Jesus. This is early in his ministry. You have known him for only a few weeks. Here is the scene:

The Compassion of Jesus & Commissioning of the Twelve

Mt. 9:35-38,10:1-15:

Jesus went around to all the towns and villages, teaching in their synagogues, proclaiming the gospel of the kingdom, and curing every disease and illness. At the sight of the crowds, his heart was moved with pity for them because they were troubled and abandoned, like sheep without a shepherd. Then he said to his disciples, "The harvest is abundant but the laborers are few; so ask the master of the harvest to send out laborers for his harvest."

Then he summoned his twelve disciples and gave them authority over unclean spirits to drive them out and to cure every disease and every illness. The names of the twelve apostles are these: first, Simon called Peter, and his brother Andrew;

James, the son of Zebedee, and his brother John; Philip and Bartholomew, Thomas and Matthew the tax collector; James, the son of Alphaeus, and Thaddeus; Simon the Cananean, and Judas Iscariot who betrayed him.

Jesus sent out these twelve after instructing them thus, "Do not go into pagan territory or enter a Samaritan town. Go rather to the lost sheep of the house of Israel. As you go, make this proclamation: 'The kingdom of heaven is at hand. Cure the sick, raise the dead, cleanse lepers, drive out demons. Without cost you have received; without cost you are to give.

Read the passage two or three times, memorizing the flow of events, and paying attention to details or phrases that stand out to you. As described on page 9 in the Introduction, creatively imagine yourself in this scene using all five senses.

You are one of Jesus's apostles. For a few weeks now, he's not called anyone else. It's just you twelve, camping at night, visiting towns by day. Jesus is, without a doubt, the biggest name in all of Israel. Thousands want to see him, to hear him, and especially to be healed by him. Many days, crowd control is your primary job. Today is particularly bad. You've found yourselves in a large clearing at the edge of a town, and it seems every poor soul with any sickness has gathered: the blind, deformed, crippled, and diseased. It smells terrible. It will take hours for Jesus to touch each person, and you'll be forced to hold people back, wrangle with the unwashed, pushy, desperate poor. You look around at the other apostles and you can tell they'd rather be elsewhere.

As usual, though, Jesus sees everything differently. You know him a little now, and you are learning to read the emotions on his face. Right now his brows are furrowed as he gazes at the crowd. Tears are forming in his eyes. He turns and looks at you directly, saying with emotion in his voice: "The harvest is abundant." The words are full of meaning. He doesn't see these

36

people as burdens or lost causes. He sees souls with promise, people born to love and be loved. You realize your heart is all wrong. You've been seeing everything backwards. Did he not say he came for the sick and sinful? Did he not heal *you*? Did he not choose you as a companion in this mission?

That night you find a place to camp, as usual. In the morning, you're the first up. You make a fire, cook breakfast. Everyone's there now, circling the fire as the sun rises. You look around at your companions' faces: Peter, James, John, and the rest. Just a few weeks ago, they were strangers, but now they are brothers. "What town today?" you ask the Lord, already imagining another grueling day. "Today will be different," he says. As of today, he explains, you're no longer backstage. You'll be doing the healing.

For a moment, imagine the nervousness of that morning as you embark with just one companion to visit towns on your own. Are you ready? Are you eager? What will you say? What will you do? How will the people react to you? What else do you feel?

...

Now return to the parish of the last Holy Hour's meditation, where you are pastor. It's Lent, and tonight you'll be helping at a penance service at a rural parish. You pack your purple stole and make the 40-minute drive. Five other priests are there, shuffling into the sacristy, out of the cold wind. A couple are your friends; the others are a lot different than you. Conversation is good, though. Despite the differences in age, in theological outlooks, you feel a brotherhood as you vest.

Now imagine, with as much detail as you can, how you sit in a corner of the church, in a hard chair, as a dozen people come to you to confess their sins and receive absolution. They are ordinary people with ordinary problems, though some carry extraordinary burdens. Over the years, you have learned that you feel most like a priest while in the confessional. When you are forgiving, consoling, counseling, it is not hard to understand that priests act *in persona Christi*, in the person of Christ. In the confessional, it is not hard to imagine you have been truly commissioned by him for this work, just like the apostles.

There's only one person left in your line, a young man of about 23, looking nervous and burdened. "Bless me, father, for I have sinned. It has been five years since my last confession...." He proceeds to pour his sins out of his heart. As he speaks, tears in his eyes, contrition in his voice, you realize that when you were his age, you committed every sin he is confessing. You remember God's mercy towards you when you most needed it. It came through the hands and words of your parish priest. Now, yourself an emissary of Christ's mercy, what do you tell this man; how do you counsel him?

Now imagine your arm raised, saying the words of absolution:

God the Father of mercies, through the death and resurrection of his Son has reconciled the world to himself and sent the Holy Spirit among us for the forgiveness of sins; through the ministry of the Church may God give you pardon and peace, and I absolve you from your sins in the name of the Father, and of the Son and of the Holy Spirit. Amen.

Colloquy

Come back to the present. Gaze at our Lord in the Blessed Sacrament. Ask him if he is calling you to be a priest, a forgiver of sins, a healer of souls. Ask imploringly, expecting an answer. Understand you likely will not hear a voice, but rather, a peacefulness of soul as you pray. Knock at the door of heaven. Listen to his response.

Write about your prayer

Use a notebook to write down your reflections. Your notes will be very important later as you revisit your discernment process.

1. Images. In this meditation, what was the most powerful thing you saw, heard, touched, smelled, or tasted? What did God show you through this?

2. Realizations. In reflecting on this passage, what did you realize about forgiveness, healing, or confession?

3. Discernment: What insights did God give you about your vocation? Can you see yourself as a priest?

4. Resolutions. What is Jesus asking you to do, concretely and specifically, as a result of this meditation? When and how will you do it?

CELEBRATING THE EUCHARIST

In this Holy Hour, meditate on how the Holy Mass re-presents the sacrifice of Jesus on the cross. Imagine being a priest celebrating Mass, and thus entering into this unfathomable mystery.

This Holy Hour has two parts of imaginative prayer. In the first part, you will be a witness to the crucifixion, paying special attention to Jesus carrying his cross. You will stand at the foot of his cross with Mary, then see the blood and water pour from his side. In the second part, you will imagine yourself as a priest, at your home parish, celebrating Mass. (Note that you may need a little extra time to thoroughly make this prayer.)

In preparation, recall the basic truth of Christianity: that Jesus Christ has won our eternal salvation through his death and resurrection. Without his death on the cross, the world would continue in its misery, cut off from communion with God. But because of his sacrifice, we have joyful hope of eternal happiness.

As you read the scripture, pay close attention to every detail.

The Crucifixion of Jesus and the Blood and Water from His Side
John 19:16b-37

So they took Jesus, and carrying the cross himself he went out to what is called the Place of the Skull, in Hebrew, Golgotha. There they crucified him, and with him two others, one on either side, with Jesus in the middle. Pilate also had an inscription written and put on the cross. It read, "Jesus the Nazorean, the King of the Jews." Now many of the Jews read this inscription, because the place where Jesus was crucified was near the city; and it was written in Hebrew, Latin, and Greek. So the chief priests of the Jews said to Pilate, "Do not write 'The King of the Jews,' but that he said, 'I am the King of the Jews.'" Pilate answered, "What I have written, I have written."

When the soldiers had crucified Jesus, they took his clothes and divided them into four shares, a share for each soldier. They also took his tunic, but the tunic was seamless, woven in one piece from the top down. So they said to one another, "Let's not tear it, but cast lots for it to see whose it will be," in order that the passage of scripture might be fulfilled that says:

"They divided my garments among them,

and for my vesture they cast lots."

This is what the soldiers did.

Standing by the cross of Jesus were his mother and his mother's sister, Mary the wife of Clopas, and Mary of Magdala. When Jesus saw his mother and the disciple there whom he loved, he said to his mother, "Woman, behold, your son." Then he said to the disciple, "Behold, your mother." And from that hour the disciple took her into his home.

After this, aware that everything was now finished, in order that the scripture might be fulfilled, Jesus said, "I thirst." There was a vessel filled with common wine. So they put a sponge soaked in wine on a sprig of hyssop and put it up to his mouth. When Jesus had taken the wine, he said, "It is finished." And bowing his head, he handed over the spirit.

Now since it was preparation day, in order that the bodies might not remain on the cross on the sabbath, for the sabbath day of that week was a solemn one, the Jews asked Pilate that their legs be broken and they be taken down. So the soldiers came and broke the legs of the first and then of the other one who was crucified with Jesus. But when they came to Jesus and saw that he was already dead, they did not break his legs, but one soldier thrust his lance into his side, and immediately blood and water flowed out. An eyewitness has testified, and his testimony is true; he knows that he is speaking the truth, so that you also may come to believe. For this happened so that the scripture passage might be fulfilled:

"Not a bone of it will be broken."

And again another passage says:

"They will look upon him whom they have pierced."

Read the passage two or three times, memorizing the flow of events, and paying attention to details or phrases that stand out to you. Then, as described on page 9 in the Introduction, creatively imagine yourself in these scenes using all five senses. Note that your imaginative prayer can go in any direction the Holy Spirit leads.

You could perhaps imagine yourself as the apostle John, the youngest apostle. In many ways, you have come of age these past three years as you have followed Jesus. But the "good old times" of walking around Israel, watching Jesus preach and heal, seem to have passed. Now everything is ruined. Last night was the most powerful Passover you had ever celebrated, but it ended the worst possible way. They've arrested Jesus.

The next day, the apostles are gone, you don't know where. But you can't leave; you have to find out what's happening to Jesus. The awful truth ripples out as the report spreads: he's been sentenced to death. You push through the crowds near the Roman praetorium. When you break through the mass of bodies and can finally see what the commotion is all about, you can barely believe the horror of the scene. Your closest friend, your teacher and Lord, is bloody beyond all recognition, and they are cruelly hoisting the cross onto his back. Hear the shouts, see the splintered wood dig into his back, his blood dripping into the dust. Follow him, step by step, as he makes his way to Golgotha.

Imagine the entire scene: the soldiers cruelly mistreating him, the nails driven through his hands and feet, his wrecked body hoisted high on the cross.

You have found Mary and her companions. Your eyes meet. As torn and hollow as you feel, you see that the depth of her pain is a thousand times worse. Her son is there, hanging in agony, naked, bleeding to death in front of a crowd. There's nothing to do. All seems lost. You stand beneath the cross together. Through bloody and cracked lips, Jesus speaks, his voice croaking, giving Mary into your care. She's your mother now.

Imagine the scene as he drinks the wine from a sponge. Hear his voice: "It is finished." Stay there with Mary, beneath her dead son.

The soldiers come, rough and rude. You hear the crack of bones as they break the legs of the criminals beside Jesus. You brace yourself as they come to Jesus, barely believing it is ending like this. A soldier makes a sudden cruel thrust with his long spear, and the blood and water gush from Christ's side. Stay there, see everything.

...

Before going on to the next meditation, reflect for a moment that Christ's sacrifice on the cross is made present at Holy Mass. As the Catechism explains:

"In the liturgical celebration of these events, they become in a certain way present and real.... When the Church celebrates the Eucharist, she commemorates Christ's Passover, and it is made present: the sacrifice Christ offered once for all on the cross remains ever present....

The sacrifice of Christ and the sacrifice of the Eucharist are one single sacrifice: The victim is one and the same: the same now offers through the ministry of priests, who then offered himself on the cross; only the manner of offering is different."

~CCC 1362-1367

...

Now imagine you are a priest, a happy priest. You are at your parish, preparing to celebrate Mass on a great Marian feast day. In the sacristy, you pull over your head a magnificent vestment embroidered with Marian symbols. You feel close to her when you wear this.

Standing at the back of the church, you are about to process. The music is playing, the altar server is lifting the cross. As you process down the center of the church, your eyes are fixed upon the huge crucifix behind the altar.

Imagine celebrating Mass, beginning in the name of the Father, and the Son, and the Holy Spirit. Imagine leading the penitential rite, the gloria. Imagine proclaiming the Gospel, touching the thick pages of the book. Now receive the gifts of bread and wine, smiling at the family who has brought them up. Imagine as many details of Mass as you wish.

Now it is the Eucharistic prayer, and you stand at the altar. Concentrate as you pick up the bread from the sacred vessel, grasping it with both hands, bending low over it. Imagine saying the words:

"Take this, all of you, and eat of it, for this is my body, which will be given up for you."

Raise the Eucharist high, for the people to see, for the Father to accept.

Now take the chalice. Feel its surprising weight. Let your fingers feel its intricate engravings. Bend low, smelling the wine, as you say:

"Take this, all of you, and drink from it, for this is the chalice of my blood, the blood of the new and eternal covenant, which will be poured out for you and for many for the forgiveness of sins. Do this in memory of me."

Colloquy

Time stops as you hold the chalice filled with Christ's blood. The crucifix behind the altar looms over you. You are gazing into the gleaming gold vessel and glimpse your own reflection in the dark red liquid. Here is a mystical moment: you are both at Mass and at calvary; you are both the priest and Christ; you are both present in the church and present before the Father in heaven.

Now raise the chalice high, your arms stretched to heaven. You hear the bells ringing. In this moment, what is in your heart of hearts? What does the Father say to his son?

Write about your prayer

Use a notebook to write down your reflections. Your notes will be very important later as you revisit your discernment process.

1. **Images**. During this prayer, what was the most powerful experience? Is there an image you can return to later in prayer? What was it?

2. **Realizations**. Did you come to any new understanding? About Christ, about Mass, about yourself? What was it?

3. **Discernment**. When you think of the possibility of priesthood, can you see yourself as a priest? How would you celebrate Mass? How would you want to live your priesthood?

4. **Resolutions**. What is Jesus asking you to do, concretely and specifically, as a result of this meditation? When and how will you do it?

OVERCOMING FEAR

In this Holy Hour, meditate on overcoming your fears by keeping your eyes fixed on Jesus.

In preparation, take as long as ten minutes to write down all your fears about entering seminary and becoming a priest—if that were indeed your vocation. Write down everything in a bulleted list. If you are afraid of celibacy, write it down. If you are afraid of telling your parents, state it. Get it all out on paper: your fear of not being accepted should you apply to seminary, or your picture being on the seminarian poster, your fear of public speaking—anything that disturbs your peace when you imagine the future.

Now put your journal aside and read the scripture:

Jesus Walks on Water and Calls Peter to Himself

Matthew 14:22-33

Then he made the disciples get into the boat and precede him to the other side, while he dismissed the crowds. After doing so, he went up on the mountain by himself to pray. When it was evening he was there alone. Meanwhile the boat, already a few miles offshore, was being tossed about by the waves, for the wind was against it.

During the fourth watch of the night, he came toward them, walking on the sea. When the disciples saw him walking on the sea they were terrified. "It is a ghost," they said, and they cried out in fear. At once Jesus spoke to them, "Take courage, it is I; do not be afraid." Peter said to him in reply, "Lord, if it is you, command me to come to you on the water." He said, "Come." Peter got out of the boat and began to walk on the water toward Jesus. But when he saw how strong the wind was he became frightened; and, beginning to sink, he cried out, "Lord, save me!" Immediately Jesus stretched out his hand and caught him, and said to him, "O you of little faith, why did you doubt?"

After they got into the boat, the wind died down. Those who were in the boat did him homage, saying, "Truly, you are the Son of God."

Read the passage two or three times, memorizing the flow of events, and paying attention to details or phrases that stand out to you. Then, as described on page 9 in the Introduction, creatively imagine yourself in these scenes using all five senses.

In this meditation, imagine yourself as Peter. Following Jesus has become much harder in recent weeks. The vitriol from the Pharisees has gotten worse. Just recently, Herod murdered Jesus's cousin John. Despite the incredible miracles you have witnessed, you are realizing there is another side to following Jesus—a dangerous side. You feel secure when you're close at his side, but at other times, fear creeps into your mind.

Tonight the teacher seems tired and wants to be alone. It's not the first time. He says he will meet you at the other side of the sea of Galilee. With the others, you clamber down the hillside to the water. Your old fishing boat is still there. The night is clear, with a bright moon, but windy. Working with the others, you've hoisted the sail and are making good time across the water, but the wind is kicking up. It's really howling now. Even as a seasoned fisherman, you're finding it difficult to navigate.

Suddenly one of the others cries out and thrusts a finger toward the shore you've just left. In the moonlight, among the waves, someone seems to be... walking? It is an eerie sight, unearthly, chilling. The figure gets closer and closer. You and your companions are terrified.

The figure is not far away when you hear his voice: "Take courage, it is I; do not be afraid." You know it is the Lord. In your bravado, you want to go to him. You put a leg out of the boat, which is still careening on the waves. Now you're walking, your eyes fixed on Jesus, walking on the water toward him. The others yell your name, in amazement but also concern. The water is cold on your bare feet. The wind is whipping your cloak, you're struggling to keep your feet. You stumble on a whitecap and look down. "What am I doing? I can't do this! This is crazy!" You're sinking. The water is at your calf, now your thighs, your waist. You look up in desperation: "Lord, save me." Jesus clasps your hand with his strong grip, pulling you up.

Colloquy

Back in the boat, you are sitting in the bow with Jesus. The wind has become only a breeze. The others are navigating while you speak alone with the Master. Talk with him about your fears; voice them aloud to him. Don't take your eyes off of him. Listen to his response.

Write about your prayer

Use a notebook to write down your reflections. Your notes will be very important later as you revisit your discernment process.

1. Images. During this prayer, what was the most powerful experience? Is there an image you can return to later in prayer? What was it?

2. Realizations. Did you come to any new understanding? About yourself or your fears? What was it?

3. Discernment: What fears do you have? With whom do you need to discuss them?

4. Resolutions. What is Jesus asking you to do, concretely and specifically, as a result of this meditation? Do you need to find a spiritual director? Who will you ask? When?

THE GRACE OF CELIBACY

In this Holy Hour, meditate on the beauty of marriage, as well as the goodness of following the Lord single-heartedly as a priest.

You will be attending the wedding at Cana as one of Jesus's disciples where you will meet a beautiful woman. You will imagine married life with her in all its fullness. You will also feel a gentle invitation from Jesus to freely follow him as one of his closest companions, as a priest. Both vocations, of course, are very good choices.

Before you begin the contemplation, though, it is critical to understand that when men begin seminary, they are not expected to have erased their desire for marriage. The Church well knows that this is impossible. Instead, through a years-long process of formation, the Church invites men to freely choose the gift of celibacy, not as a burdensome obligation required of priests, but happily, as a pathway to conforming their lives to Christ. To be ordained—after at least five or six years of training—seminarians must have gladly discovered a "celibate heart," a joy in serving the Lord above all else, leaving behind the beauty of family life for an even greater spiritual good.

Be confident that there is tremendous wisdom in the Church's insistence that her priests be unmarried—or rather, that they have the Church as their spouse. As St. Paul says, "An unmarried man is anxious about the things of the Lord, how he may please the Lord. But a married man is anxious about the things of the world, how he may please his wife." Again, both vocations are good. As St. Paul further explains, "I am telling you this for your own benefit, not to impose a restraint upon you, but for the sake of propriety and adherence to the Lord without distraction" (1 Cor 7:32-33, 35).

It is also extremely important to understand that the choice between priesthood and marriage is not a choice between sacrifice and bliss. It is true that a priest will never cuddle a toddler as he crawls back and forth from his father's lap to his mother's arms. There is true sweetness in family life. Thus foregoing the joys of family is a true sacrifice. But—and this is an aspect that many young men, in their romanticism, forget—family life also brings many burdens and crosses. The Catechism itself includes a long passage on the particular trials that have plagued the relations of men and women since the Fall (CCC 1606-1608). So as much as you feel an intense natural desire for love, sex, and family, know that these goods also require substantial sacrifice as well. Some older priests, who have heard thousands of confessions and counseled hundreds of troubled couples, find affirmation in their choice of celibacy. (Though of course, priests are also edified by witnessing many happy marriages too.) The main point is this: both marriage and priesthood have their own unique joys and require their own unique sacrifices.

With all this in mind, now turn your imagination to the wedding of Cana, where by his very presence, Jesus blessed and sanctified marriage.

The Wedding at Cana
John 2:1-12

On the third day there was a wedding in Cana in Galilee, and the mother of Jesus was there. Jesus and his disciples were also invited to the wedding. When the wine ran short, the mother of Jesus said to him, "They have no wine." And Jesus said to her, "Woman, how does your concern affect me? My hour has not yet come." His mother said to the servers, "Do whatever he tells you."

Now there were six stone water jars there for Jewish ceremonial washings, each holding twenty to thirty gallons. Jesus told them, "Fill the jars with water." So they filled them to the brim. Then he told them, "Draw some out now and take it to the headwaiter." So they took it. And when the headwaiter tasted the water that had become wine, without knowing where it came from (although the servers who had drawn the water knew), the headwaiter called the bridegroom and said to him, "Everyone serves good wine first, and then when people have drunk freely, an inferior one; but you have kept the good wine until now."

Jesus did this as the beginning of his signs in Cana in Galilee and so revealed his glory, and his disciples began to believe in him. After this, he and his mother, his brothers, and his disciples went down to Capernaum and stayed there only a few days.

Read the passage two or three times, memorizing the flow of events, and paying attention to details or phrases that stand out to you. Then, as described on page 9 in the Introduction, creatively imagine yourself in these scenes using all five senses.

In this meditation, imagine yourself as one of the disciples of Jesus. You have just recently begun following him. You are amazed and awed by his teaching, but still have much to learn of him. He and his followers have all been invited to a wedding. You and the others have washed your cloaks, trimmed your beards, and traveled with much anticipation to Cana.

The night does not disappoint. It is a lovely scene, with bowers of flowers and a tremendous spread of food, all glowing under lamplight in the courtyard. Take in the details of the scene. Hear the music, smell the roasted meat, and see the guests all attired for the great occasion.

See too the many young women who have gathered as friends of the bride. They are in a group near the wine table, chatting and laughing. You find them much more interesting than either the food or the wine. One in particular stands out. She is animatedly telling a story to the others, her dark curls framing her olive skin. Her smile is modest but playful. "Before the end of the night I will talk to her," you vow to yourself.

Now you sense some commotion on the other side of the courtyard, near where Jesus is sitting with his mother. You have only just met Mary when you arrived today, and immediately you noticed the deep love she and Jesus have for one another. Now they are speaking with the steward; it looks like Mary has steered him to Jesus' table by the elbow. You move close and overhear the whole conversation. You feel a pang of secondhand embarrassment for the family as you learn that the wine has run short so soon. There is a moment of slight tension, but then you notice a look of understanding pass between Jesus and his mother. She is inviting him to something. She turns to the steward: "Do whatever he tells you."

What follows is inconceivable to you. For twenty minutes, servants bring pitcher after pitcher of water. You see it slosh down the lip of the giant stone jars. The festivities are going on full force; only you have noticed that something is afoot. Then you see the headwaiter sample the water-turned-wine, his eyes opened wide in astonishment. You can guess what has happened, and move closer, grab a cup and dip it in the deep red liquid. As you sip, you look toward Jesus. He meets your eyes with a knowing gaze. Your amazement is total. You are suddenly profoundly awed that this man, this miracle-worker, has chosen you as a companion. You vow to follow him always. You long to know him more deeply.

The night goes on, with even further joyousness now that they have announced the new wine. Remembering your promise, you fill a cup, and mustering up some courage, walk across the courtyard, bringing it to the girl you had noticed earlier in the evening. Her smile is radiant. She almost seems to have been waiting for you. You begin with small talk that progresses into the deeper conversation about life, about love, about the future.

...

Step out of the wedding at Cana now and spend several minutes imagining your own future if God called you to marriage. Have a "holy fantasy" of falling in love, having a big wedding, and starting a family. Imagine the details of holding your first child, witnessing her First Holy Communion, cheering at graduation, and one day walking her down the aisle. Imagine growing old with your wife, having grandchildren, and sharing all the poignant moments of their childhoods. Acknowledge all the goodness and beauty of married life.

...

Come back to Cana now. It is late and the wedding is winding down. The hours you've spent with this beautiful young woman seem to have passed in minutes. Her eyes and smile are the most beautiful things you have ever seen. Her friends are gathering at one of the fires; it looks like they're staying later than the other guests. She asks you to join them. But your companions, Jesus's new disciples, have bumped you on the shoulder and nodded over to Jesus. It's time to go. Your heart is torn. "Wait a minute," you say to the girl.

Colloquy

You walk over to Jesus, who has been looking at you across the courtyard. He knows what's going on; he can read you like a book. His expression is difficult to interpret. On the one hand, he seems slightly amused at your amorous encounter. On the other hand, you can see he missed you; he is inviting you to be a close companion. There is no judgment in his eyes. You are perfectly free. To which of these profound vocations is Jesus calling you? They are both so attractive, but He is not calling you to both. Look into the eyes of Jesus.

You know that you will always love this man, no matter what. You will never forsake him, nor he you. You know where you can find him preaching and teaching. The question is: will you listen from the crowd, or imitate him as an apostle? You look over your shoulder to where the girl is waiting by a warm fire. What do you say to Jesus? What does he say to you?

Write about your prayer

Use a notebook to write down your reflections. Your notes will be very important later as you revisit your discernment process.

1. **Images.** During this prayer, what was the most powerful experience? Is there an image you can return to later in prayer? What was it?

2. **Realizations.** Did you come to any new understanding about marriage or celibacy? About the freedom to respond to God's call?

3. **Discernment.** Know that an attraction to family life is not necessarily a sign that you are called to marriage. With this in mind, how strong is your desire for marriage? How strong is your desire for priesthood? To which vocation do you think Jesus is inviting you?

4. **Resolutions.** What is Jesus asking you to do, concretely and specifically, as a result of this meditation?

SACRIFICING EVERYTHING

In this Holy Hour, ask Jesus directly if he is calling you to be a priest.

Your contemplation will be on Jesus's encounter with the rich young man who felt he could not follow Jesus because of the sacrifice involved. This contemplation will be very straightforward and perhaps shorter than the others.

First, however, take 10-15 minutes to review your notes from the previous eight Holy Hours. See if you find a pattern or progression of ideas and insights. Pay special attention to the colloquies: when you have spoken heart to heart with Jesus, what did he say? Spend some time revisiting the highpoints you have experienced.

...

In his book *To Save a Thousand Souls*, Fr. Brett Brannen writes, "To do anything less than the will of God for your life will bore you."

Ask yourself why you are making these Holy Hours in the first place. Is it not because your heart is restless? Is it not because you sense a call to something more? You are rightly repulsed by a life of boredom. You instead long for a life of meaning. Deep down, you want Jesus to call you to something big, something hard, something heroic. The only things holding you back are fears of inadequacy, fears of missing out on a different life, and fears of the pain of sacrifice.

Mindful of these fears, and yet yearning for something more, read the scripture.

Jesus Encounters a Rich Young Man

Matthew 19:16-22

Now someone approached him and said, "Teacher, what good must I do to gain eternal life?" He answered him, "Why do you ask me about the good? There is only One who is good. If you wish to enter into life, keep the commandments." He asked him, "Which ones?" And Jesus replied, "'You shall not kill; you shall not commit adultery; you shall not steal; you shall not bear false witness; honor your father and your mother'; and 'you shall love your neighbor as yourself.'" The young man said to him, "All of these I have observed. What do I still lack?"

Jesus said to him, "If you wish to be perfect, go, sell what you have and give to the poor, and you will have treasure in heaven. Then come, follow me." When the young man heard this statement, he went away sad, for he had many possessions.

Read the passage two or three times, memorizing the flow of events, and paying attention to details or phrases that stand out to you. Then, as described on page 9 in the Introduction, creatively imagine yourself in these scenes using all five senses.

In this meditation, you are the rich young man. You have been following Jesus from afar. You have been at the edge of the crowds and witnessed his miracles. You have heard his words, and they have lit a fire in your heart. You have seen how, at the end of the day, he withdraws with a small band of followers. You have wondered what it is like to be among them.

Already in your life, you are striving for holiness, at times with difficulty, it is true, but those who know you would say you are a good man.

But isn't there something more? Today you resolve to speak, personally, with the teacher. To ask him directly what to do with your life. Imagine approaching him. He is walking along the seashore, apart from his followers. You are walking behind him, your feet crunching in the sand, the wind on your face. You see the back of his cloak. From behind, he seems just an ordinary man. "Teacher, teacher!" you call out. He turns to you. His gaze is not at all ordinary. It is full of love, but also with purpose. He knows you, knows your future. You can trust his every word.

Colloquy

Speak to Jesus from your heart. Speak to him about your struggle with holiness, about keeping the commandments. Tell him about your attraction to the priesthood, your excitement that he may be calling you, as well as your fear that he may be calling. Ask him, "What should I do with my life? Are you calling me to be your priest?" Know that he always respects your freedom—but know, too, that he has a plan. Spend time listening for his response.

When the conversation is done, what emotion do you feel? Are you peaceful or excited? Or do you walk away sad?

Write about your prayer

Use a notebook to write down your reflections. Your notes will be very important later as you revisit your discernment process.

1. **Images.** During this prayer, what was the most powerful experience? Is there an image you can return to later in prayer? What was it?

2. **Realizations.** Did you come to any new understanding about the different levels of discipleship? About Jesus' invitation to a more radical life?

3. **Discernment:** Do you think Jesus is calling you to be a priest? In the course of these Holy Hours, has there been a consistent message, theme, or emotion? What is it?

4. **Resolutions.** Regardless of the vocation to which you are called, what is your next step? If you have heard a call to the priesthood, whom should you contact? What should you do? When?

ARRIVING AT AN ANSWER

How will you know that you have found God's will? How can you be certain that you have reached the clarity you seek? When you feel freedom to move forward.

Fr. Timothy Gallagher, an expert on discernment, writes:

"Absence of an answer inhibits freedom for action; a clear answer brings peace of heart and releases energy for service."

In other words, if you have prepared well by seeking Jesus first above all things, and you have also discerned well, noting the movement of your heart during times of peaceful prayer, then when you reach a good decision, you should feel freedom and joy in pursuing it.

Your vocation is like fruit on a tree. If you try to pick it too soon, it will harm both the tree and the fruit, and it will not taste good. But if it stays on the tree too long, it will rot. Your discernment is both about what God wants you to do, and *when* He wants you to do it.

When not to make a decision

Do not make a decision about your vocation if you feel lowness of spirit, darkness of soul, a lack of hope, or generally feel slothful and sad. This is often the work of the Enemy. When you are feeling down and depressed, or spiritually anxious and worried, postpone any decision until you regain a measure of spiritual peace.

Likewise, do not make a decision about the priesthood without guidance from a priest or spiritual mentor. He who counsels himself has a fool for a spiritual director. Thoroughly discuss the results of your Holy Hours with a wise guide who can help interpret your experience.

Realize, too, that you may need more time. Sometimes the Lord says "yes." Sometimes he says "no." And sometimes he says "not yet." However, do not use this as an excuse. If you postpone a decision, be certain it is for good reason. Do not delay because of laziness or fear.

Moving toward the priesthood

It is impossible to become a priest without speaking to the Vocation Director. He is the emissary of the bishop, the voice of the Church. He must get to know you, your background, and your strengths and weaknesses. If he confirms that God seems to be calling you, he will guide you through the process of applying to seminary. Whether or not you are accepted as a seminarian, he will guide you with a priestly heart. So if you feel God could be calling you to the priesthood, even if you are uncertain, contact the Vocation Director immediately. Do it today, this very hour.

The fruit of a good discernment

What is the benefit of a thorough, God-centered discernment? You will have reassurance in times of future doubt. If you have completed the Holy Hours well—and especially if you have kept a journal along the way—when future times of doubt and difficulty arise, you can look back and say, "I really did my best to discern well, and the Lord brought me to this place. I know I am where God wants me to be."